Community Workers

Protecting Your Home

A Book About Firefighters

Ann Owen
Illustrated by Eric Thomas

T0084853

Thanks to our advisers for their expertise, research, knowledge, and advice:

George Burke, Assistant to the General President
International Association of Fire Fighters, Washington, D.C.

Susan Kesselring, M.A., Literacy Educator
Rosemount-Apple Valley-Eagan (Minnesota) School District

PICTURE WINDOW BOOKS
Minneapolis, Minnesota

Managing Editor: Bob Temple
Creative Director: Terri Foley
Editor: Peggy Henrikson
Editorial Adviser: Andrea Cascardi
Copy Editor: Laurie Kahn
Designer: John Moldstad
Page production: Picture Window Books
The illustrations in this book were prepared digitally.

Picture Window Books
1710 Roe Crest Drive
North Mankato, MN 56003
www.capstonepub.com

Copyright © 2004 by Picture Window Books, a Capstone imprint.
All rights reserved. No part of this book may be reproduced without written permission from the publisher.
The publisher takes no responsibility for the use of any of the materials or methods described in this book, nor for the products thereof.

Library of Congress Cataloging-in-Publication Data
Owen, Ann, 1953–
Protecting your home : a book about firefighters / written by Ann Owen ; illustrated by Eric Thomas.
p. cm. — (Community workers)
Summary: Describes some of the things that firefighters do to help protect people and their homes.
Includes bibliographical references and index.
ISBN 978-1-4048-0088-5 (library binding)
ISBN 978-1-4048-0482-1 (paperback)
1. Fire protection engineering—Juvenile literature. 2. Rescue work—Juvenile literature.
3. Firefighters—Juvenile literature. [1. Fire extinction. 2. Firefighters. 3. Occupations.]
I. Thomas, Eric, ill. II. Title. III. Community workers (Picture Window Books)
TH9148 .O94 2004
628.9'2—dc21
                                                                         2003004214

Many people
in your community
have jobs helping others.

What do firefighters do?

Firefighters teach you
to stop, drop, and roll.

drop, and roll

Firefighters keep their trucks clean
and their equipment ready.

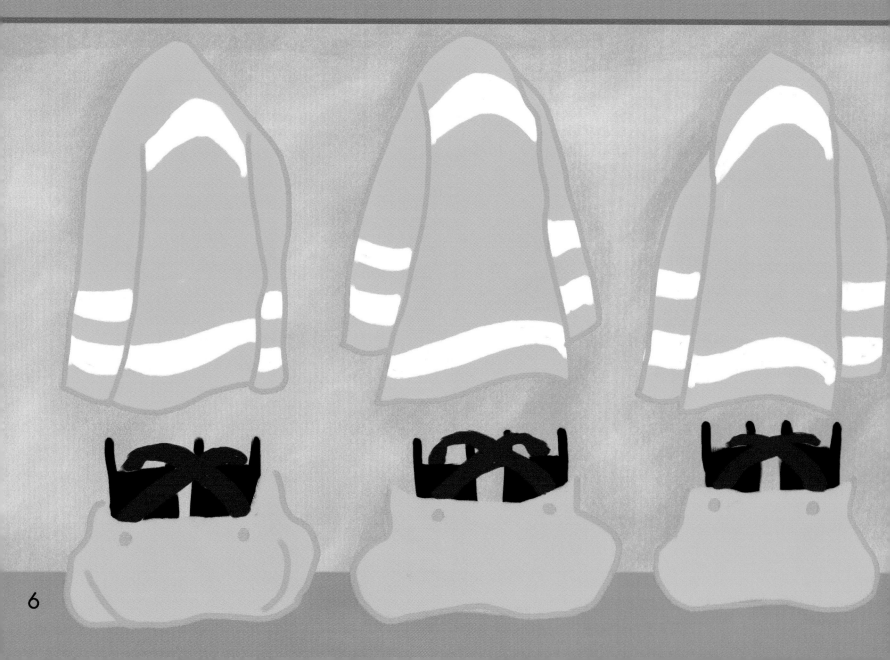

Firefighters hurry to help

There's a fire at Oak and Main.

with flashing lights and loud sirens.

10

and special masks.

Firefighters climb ladders,

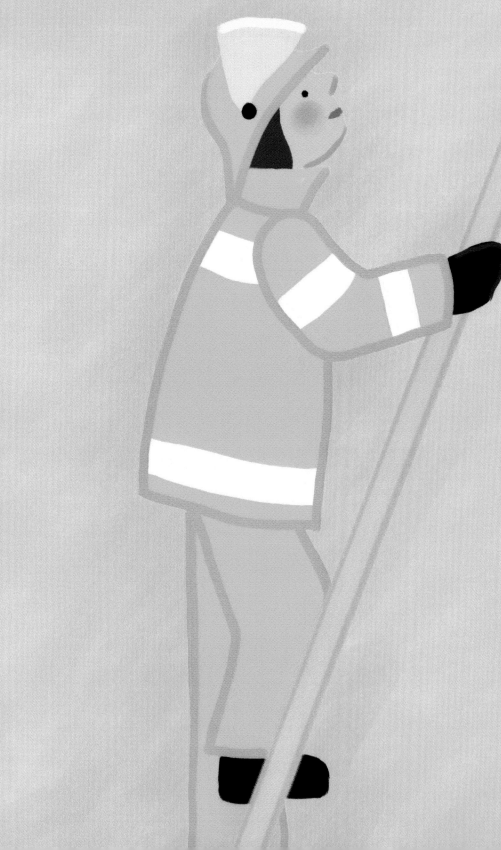

spray water,

and use tools.

Firefighters rescue people

Don't worry. You're going to be just fine.

from all kinds of danger.

Firefighters rush in and
make sure everyone gets out.

Thank you
for saving Timber!

They save pets, too.

Firefighters protect tall buildings,

thick forests,

and grassy fields.

Firefighters protect your home.

Make sure you check your smoke alarm.

Did You Know?

- Firefighters teach you to stop, drop, and roll if your clothing ever catches on fire. Rolling on the ground puts the fire out.

- The long ladders (called aerial ladders) on fire trucks can reach up about 100 feet (31 meters). This is as high as the 10th floor of a building.

- Many fire departments used to keep dogs at the firehouses. Dalmatians were the most popular firehouse dogs. Firefighters first kept and trained dalmatians back when fire trucks were pulled by horses. The dalmatians protected the horses from stray dogs. The spotted, black-and-white dalmatians were easy for the horses to recognize through smoke. The dogs also were used to catch mice in the firehouses.

- Most fire trucks are red. Yellow fire trucks also are common. The Grapeville, Pennsylvania, Fire Department has purple fire trucks.

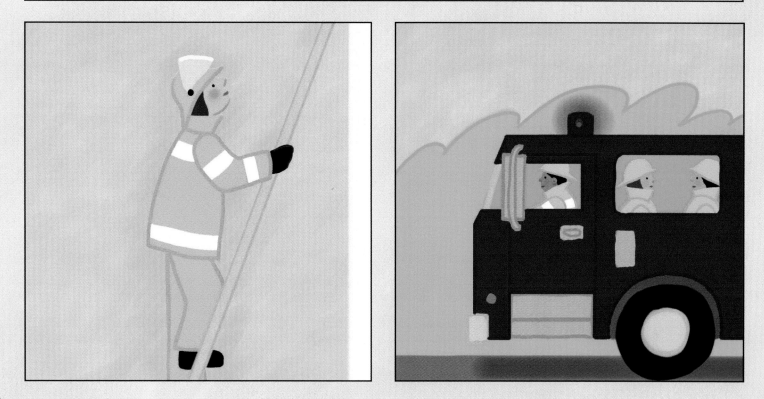

A Firefighter's Equipment

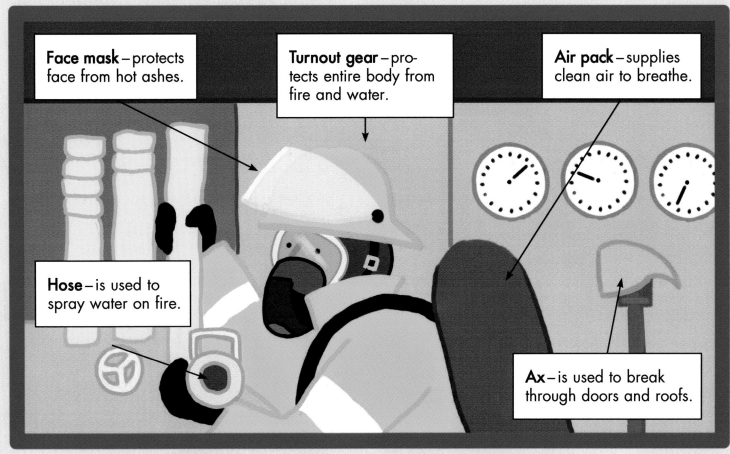

Face mask—protects face from hot ashes.

Turnout gear—protects entire body from fire and water.

Air pack—supplies clean air to breathe.

Hose—is used to spray water on fire.

Ax—is used to break through doors and roofs.

Words to Know

air pack (AIR PAK)—a tank of air that firefighters wear in smoke so they can breathe

community (kuh-MYOO-nuh-tee)—a group of people who live in the same area

equipment (i-KWIP-muhnt)—tools, machines, and special clothing needed to do a job

protect (pruh-TEKT)—to keep safe from danger

rescue (RESS-kyoo)—to save, or to get something or someone out of danger

siren (SYE-ruhn)—something that makes a loud, high noise to warn people. Fire trucks have sirens to warn people that the trucks are coming through fast.

turnout gear (TURN-out GIHR)—the clothing and equipment that firefighters wear to a fire. Heavy, layered clothes help protect a firefighter's body from fire and water.

To Learn More

More Books to Read

Bowman-Kruhm, Mary and Claudine G. Wirths. *A Day in the Life of a Firefighter*. New York: PowerKids Press, 1997.

Klingel, Cynthia and Robert B. Noyed. *Firefighters*. Chanhassen, Minn.: Child's World, 2002.

Ready, Dee. *Fire Fighters*. Mankato, Minn.: Bridgestone Books, 1997.

Royston, Angela. *Fire Fighter!* New York: DK Pub., 1998.

Schaefer, Lola M. *We Need Fire Fighters*. Mankato, Minn.: Pebble Books, 2000.

Index